I0160070

Table of Contents

Practical Guide to the Operational Use of the UZI Submachine Gun

By Erik Lawrence

Copyright ©2014 Erik Lawrence

Printed and bound in the United States of America

First printing 2012
Second printing 2014

ISBN-10: 1-941998-18-6
ISBN-13: 978-1-941998-18-2
EBOOK – ISBN-13: 978-1-941998-36-6
LCCN:

ATTENTION US MILITARY UNITS, US GOVERNMENT AGENCIES AND PROFESSIONAL ORGANIZATIONS: Quantity discounts are available on bulk purchases of this book. Special books or book excerpts can also be created to fit specific needs. For information, please contact:

Erik Lawrence
erik@vig-sec.com

CREDITS:
Wikipedia contributors, "Main Page," Wikipedia, The Free Encyclopedia,
http://en.wikipedia.org/w/index.php?title=Main_Page&oldid=83971314
(accessed October 9, 2012).

Firearms are potentially dangerous and must be handled responsibly by individuals. The technical information presented in this manual on the use of the UZI Submachine Gun reflects the author's research, beliefs, and experiences. The information in this book is presented for academic study only. Neither the author nor the publisher assumes any responsibility for the use or misuse of information contained in this book.

SAFETY NOTICE
Before starting an inspection, ensure the weapon is cleared. Do not manipulate the trigger until the weapon has been cleared of all ammunition. Inspect the chamber to ensure that it is empty and no ammunition is present. Keep the weapon oriented in a safe direction when loading and handling.

AMMUNITION NOTICE- This weapon fires the 9x19mm (9mm Luger) primarily but also .45 ACP and .22 LR. Firing the incorrect ammunition will damage the weapon and possibly injure the operator.

Training should be received from knowledgeable and experienced operators on this particular weapons system. Vigilant Security Services provides this training and continually perfects its instruction with up-to-date information from actual use.

www.vig-sec.com

Section 1

Introduction

The objective of this manual is to allow the reader to be able to use the Major Uziel Gal-designed UZI submachine gun (SMG) competently. The manual will give the reader background/specifications of the weapon; instructions on its operation, disassembly, and assembly; proper firing procedure; and malfunction/misfire procedures. Operator-level maintenance will also be detailed to allow the reader to understand and become competent in the use and maintenance of the UZI SMG.

Figure 1-1 UZI Designer Major Uziel Gal

Description

The Uzi (Hebrew: עוזי, officially cased as UZI) is a family of Israeli open bolt, blowback-operated submachine guns. Smaller variants are considered to be machine pistols. The Uzi was one of the first weapons to use a telescoping bolt design which allows for the magazine to be housed in the pistol grip for a shorter weapon.

The first Uzi submachine gun was designed by Major Uziel Gal in the late 1940s. The prototype was finished in 1950; first introduced to IDF special forces in 1954, the weapon were placed into general issue two years later. The Uzi has found use as a personal defense weapon by rear-echelon troops, officers, artillery troops and tankers, as well as a frontline weapon by elite light infantry assault forces.

The Uzi has been exported to over 90 countries. Over its service lifetime, it has been manufactured by Israel Military Industries, FN Herstal, and other manufacturers. From the 1960s through the 1980s, Uzi submachine guns were sold to more military and police markets than any other submachine gun ever made.

Design

The Uzi uses an open bolt, blowback-operated design quite similar to the Czech ZK 476, from which it was developed. The open bolt design exposes the breech end of the barrel, and improves cooling during periods of continuous fire; however, it means that since the bolt is held to the rear when cocked, the receiver is more susceptible to contamination from sand and dirt ingress. It and the Czechoslovak series 23 to 26 were the first weapons to use a telescoping bolt design, in which the bolt wraps around the breech end of the barrel. This allows the barrel to be moved far back into the receiver and the magazine to be housed in the pistol grip, allowing for a heavier, slower-firing bolt in a shorter, better-balanced weapon.

The weapon is constructed primarily from stamped sheet metal, making it less expensive per unit to manufacture than an equivalent design machined from forgings. With relatively few moving parts, the Uzi is easy to strip for maintenance or repair. The magazine is housed within the pistol grip, allowing for intuitive and easy reloading in dark or difficult conditions, under the principle of "hand finds hand". The pistol grip is fitted with a grip safety, making it difficult to fire accidentally. However, the protruding vertical magazine makes the gun awkward to fire when prone. The Uzi features a bayonet lug.

Controls are relatively simple. The non-reciprocating charging handle on the top of the receiver cover is used to retract the bolt. Submachine gun variants have a ratchet safety mechanism which will catch the bolt and lock its movement if it is retracted past the magazine, but not far enough to engage the sear. Semi auto civilian market versions of the Uzi usually do not have or need this feature. When the handle is fully retracted to the rear, the bolt will cock/catch on the sear mechanism and the handle can then be released to spring fully forward under power of a small spring attaching it to the top cover. It will remain forward during firing of the weapon since it does not reciprocate when the bolt is thrust backward by the force of a cartridge firing, or forward by the main action spring. The military/police versions of the Uzi will fire immediately upon chambering a cartridge as the Uzi is an open bolt weapon. This feature is extensively modified on commercial market semi auto Uzis in order to prevent fully automatic fire. The semi auto variants (whether rifle or pistol) fire from the closed bolt, with the entire bolt mechanism designed as a two-piece mechanism. The main bolt functions much like the original, but will close upon release of the charging handle. A mechanism containing part of the shape of the bolt and firing pin remains cocked to the rear. That striker like mechanism is only released forward when the trigger is pulled. Some gunsmiths in the USA have modified the semi auto mechanism to work as fully automatic, but the uses are very limited, often only found in rare "collector and law enforcement" models which were manufactured in Israel as semiautomatic but modified elsewhere.

There are two external safety mechanisms on the Uzi, one being a selector lever which includes positions for "safe" which locks the sear and prevents movement of the bolt, "semi", which is one notch forward, which will allow the weapon to function in semiautomatic single shot mode, requiring the trigger to be pulled for each shot, and then "automatic" with the selector all the way forward, which will disengage part of the sear mechanism, allowing use of the trigger to control the firing mechanism. Once on automatic, the user may hold the trigger back and the weapon will fire until the magazine is empty. The bolt will then most likely come to rest on an empty chamber once the magazines is empty since the Uzi does not employ a bolt hold open on empty magazine mechanism like those found on military weapons that fire from the closed bolt. A very rare semiautomatic version made by FN Herstal and sold in Europe for a short time during the 1970s functioned exactly the same way, but the most forward setting on the selector lever was eliminated and blocked off. That variant was not approved for commercial import into the USA and was eventually withdrawn from production after having a relatively short commercial life in Western Europe and Canada.

The second external safety mechanism is a grip safety, located at the rear of the grip and meant to help prevent accidental discharge if the weapon is dropped, or the user loses a firm grip on the weapon during firing. The grip safety on the Uzi uses a stronger spring than that found on most handguns with a somewhat similar mechanism (US M1911, German Luger). The pistol grip must be firmly held by the user in order to allow the weapon to function, regardless of any manipulation of other controls.

The trigger mechanism is a conventional firearm trigger, but functions only to control the release mechanism for either the bolt (submachine gun) or firing pin holding mechanism (semi auto) since the UZI does not incorporate any internal cocking or hammer mechanism. While the system is much more mechanically simple than say, the Heckler & Koch MP5, it creates a noticeable delay from the point the user pulls the trigger and the point that the weapon actually fires. This delay is common with weapons that fire from the "open bolt".

The magazine release button/lever is located on the lower portion of the pistol grip and is intended to be manipulated by the non-firing hand. The paddle-like button lays flush with the pistol grip in order to help prevent accidental release of the magazine during soldier maneuvers and day to day activity.

Of the two stocks employed by the IDF, the wooden stock was the simpler and more robust of the two. The wooden stock is quick-detachable through the use of a release mechanism on the bottom side. Some commercial variants of the Uzi lacked the quick release mechanism and have the stock bolted in place. The second, and by far most popular stock on the Uzi was a unique folding stock which folds under the gun. It is robust but complex and was replaced by a side folding stock on the more compact models. Neither of the folding stocks can be quickly or easily removed from the weapon.

When the gun is de-cocked (the magazine must be removed or at least lowered enough to prevent feeding a round in the chamber in order to prevent the weapon from firing when it is being de-cocked), the ejector port closes, preventing entry of dust and dirt. Though the Uzi's stamped-metal receiver is equipped with pressed reinforcement slots to accept accumulated dirt and sand, the weapon can still jam with heavy accumulations of sand in desert combat conditions when not cleaned regularly.[8] The magazine must be removed prior to "decocking" the weapon or else the bolt will feed a round when being let forward and then leave the firing pin resting on an unfired primer, which can then fire if the weapon is knocked or dropped. The decocking procedure is to remove the magazine, check the chamber (which should be empty) and then pull the trigger which will release the bolt to fall on the empty chamber. The magazine may then be re-inserted. To ready the weapon for firing again, the bolt handle must be retracted to the rear. Use of the selector switch is irrelevant to this process, except that it will prevent the bolt from moving when it is in the "safe" position.

The characteristics of the UZI SMG

Figure 1-2 UZI

A. Country of Origin: Israel

B. Military Designation: UZI

C. Operation: Full- and semi-automatic fire

D. Cartridge: 9x19mm and (.45 ACP and .22 LR – Civilian conversions)

E. Length:

 a. Extended: 25 inches (640mm)

 b. Collapsed: 18.5 inches (470mm)

F. Barrel: 10.2 inches (260mm)

G. Weight

 a. SMG: 7.7 lbs. (3.5kg) Unloaded

 b. Stick magazine – 20, 25, 32, 40, and 50 rounds

H. Type of Feed: 20, 25, 32, 40, 50-round detachable box

I. Operating System: Blowback, open bolt

J. Rate of Fire: 600 rpm

K. Maximum Effective Range: 200 meters

Figure 1-7 Photo for the folding stock and wooden stock UZI variants

Figure 1-7 Photo of the UZI with stock folded

Mini-UZI

Figure 1-17a Mini-UZI with shoulder stock folded

Figure 1-17b Mini-UZI with shoulder stock extended

Caliber: 9x19mm (9mm Luger)

Type: Blowback, open bolt

Overall length: Stock folded 36 cm/xx inches and extended 60 cm/xx inches

Weight unloaded: 3.7 kg/xxx pounds

Barrel length: xxx cm/xxx inches

Magazine capacity: 20-, 25-, or 32-round detachable box magazine

Rate of Fire: 950 rounds per minute (rpm)

Maximum Effective Range: 100 meters

The Mini Uzi is a scaled down version of the full size Uzi. It was introduced in 1980, but did not replace the full size Uzi in production. Due to its reduced size and lighter bolt the rate of fire is higher. The Mini Uzi is the only Uzi that is available in both the open and closed bolt designs.

Micro-UZI

Figure 1-18a Micro-UZI with shoulder stock folded

Figure 1-18b Micro-UZI with shoulder stock extended

Caliber: 9x19mm (9mm Luger)

Type: Blowback, open bolt

Overall length: Stock folded 25 cm/xx inches and extended 46 cm/xx inches

Weight unloaded: 1.5 kg/3.3 pounds

Barrel length: 11.7 cm/4.5 inches

Magazine capacity: 20-round detachable box magazine

Rate of Fire: 1250 rounds per minute (rpm)

Maximum Effective Range: 30 meters

The Micro Uzi is the smallest version of the Uzi family. It was introduced in 1982, only two years after the Mini Uzi. Due to its reduced size and lighter bolt the rate of fire is much higher. The Pistol Uzi is a semi-automatic fire version of the Micro Uzi. The barrel is also slightly shorter and no shoulder stock is fitted. The Para

Uzi was produced very briefly in the 1990's. It has an angled pistol grip as it uses Glock magazines instead of Uzi ones and an accessory rail is mounted on top of the weapon.

Background

The Uzi gun was designed by Major (Captain at the time) Uziel Gal of the Israel Defense Forces (IDF) following the 1948 Arab-Israeli War. The weapon was submitted to the Israeli army for evaluation and won out over more conventional designs due to its simplicity and economy of manufacture. Gal did not want the weapon to be named after him, but his request was ignored. The Uzi was officially adopted in 1951. First introduced to IDF Special Forces in 1954, the weapon was placed into general issue two years later. The first Uzis were equipped with a short, fixed wooden buttstock, and this is the version that initially saw combat during the 1956 Suez campaign, (Figure 1-3). Later models would be equipped with a folding metal stock.

Figure 1-3 IDF troop in 1956 with the UZI

The Uzi was used as a personal defense weapon by rear-echelon troops, officers, artillery troops and tankers, as well as a frontline weapon by elite light infantry assault forces. The Uzi's compact size and firepower proved instrumental in clearing Syrian bunkers and Jordanian defensive positions during the 1967 Six-Day War. Though the weapon was phased out of frontline IDF service in the 1980s, some Uzis and Uzi variants were still used by a few IDF units until December 2003, when the IDF announced that it was retiring the Uzi from all IDF forces. It was subsequently replaced by the fully automatic Micro Tavor.

Figure 1-4 UZI in the Sinai campaign

In general, the Uzi was a reliable weapon in military service. However, even the Uzi fell victim to extreme conditions of sand and dust. During the Sinai campaign of the Yom Kippur War, (Figure 1-4) the IDF army units reaching the Suez reported that of all their small arms, only the 7.62 mm FN MAG machine gun was still in operation.

Figure 1-5 UZI in the hands of the infantry

The Uzi proved especially useful for mechanized infantry needing a compact weapon, and for infantry units clearing bunkers and other confined spaces, (Figure 1-5). However, its limited range and accuracy in automatic fire (approximately 50m) could be disconcerting when encountering enemy forces armed with longer-range small arms, and heavier support weapons could not always substitute for a longer-ranged individual weapon. These failings eventually caused the phase-out of the Uzi from IDF forces.

Figure 1-6 Liberian with a UZI in Monrovia

The Uzi has been used in various conflicts by terrorists and criminals outside Israel and the Middle East during the 1960s to present, (Figure 1-6).

Nomenclature

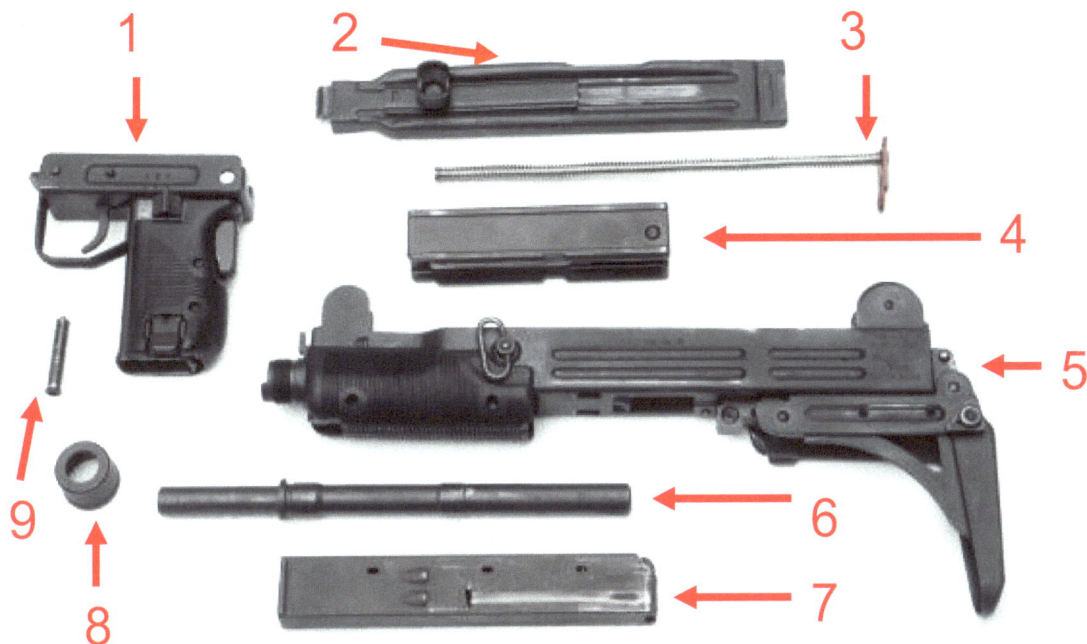

Figure 1-7 Photo of the disassembled UZI SMG

1- Pistol Grip Assembly
2- Top Cover
3- Operating Rod and Spring
4- Bolt
5- Receiver Assembly

6- Barrel
7- Magazine
8- Barrel Nut
9- Takedown Pin

Stick Magazine Nomenclature

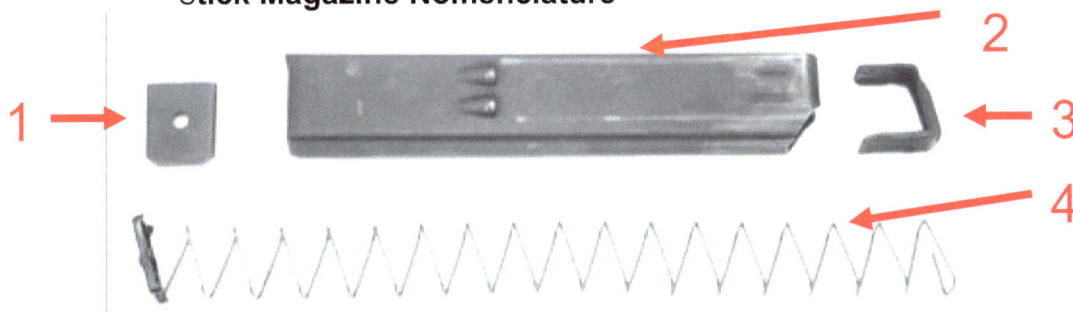

Figure1-15 Stick Magazine Nomenclature

1- Floorplate   2- Body   3- Follower   4- Spring

Operation

Clearing the UZI SMG

Figure 2-2a UZI on SAFE

A. Ensure the UZI is on S = "SAFE," and pointed in a safe direction.

Figure 2-3a Depress magazine release

Figure 2-3b Remove magazine

B. Remove the magazine by pressing in on the bottom of the magazine release lever (Figure 2-3a) and pull the magazine from the magazine well (Figure 2-3b). Place the magazine in a magazine pouch or set it down.

Figure 2-2a Bolt to the rear

C. If the bolt is locked to the rear; look into the ejection port to visually check the chamber to ensure there is no round in the chamber that failed to be extracted and ejected (Figures 2-4a).

Figure 2-5

D. If the bolt is forward you will need to pull the cocking handle to the rear and then look in the ejection port to visually inspect the chamber to ensure there is no round in the chamber that failed to be extracted and ejected (Figure 2-5).

Figure 2-6

E. If you have ensured the magazine is removed and the chamber is clear, while holding rearward pressure on the cocking handle, press the trigger and allow the bolt to move slightly forward. Once the bolt has moved forward 1/4" let go of the trigger and continue to allow the bolt to move forward under your control (Figure 2-6).

Safety Catch and Bolt Positions

Figure 2-2a Bolt to the rear   **Figure 2-2b Bolt forward**

UZI SMG bolt positions

NOTE- remember the UZI is an open bolt firing weapon. You must remove the source of ammunition (magazine) to clear the weapon safely. Riding the bolt forward to close the bolt on a weapon with a loaded magazine will cause the weapon to fire!

Folding stock manipulation

Unfolding the stock

Figure 1-13 Stock in the folded position

Figure 1-13a   **Figure 1-13b**
Press down on the toe of the stock and pull

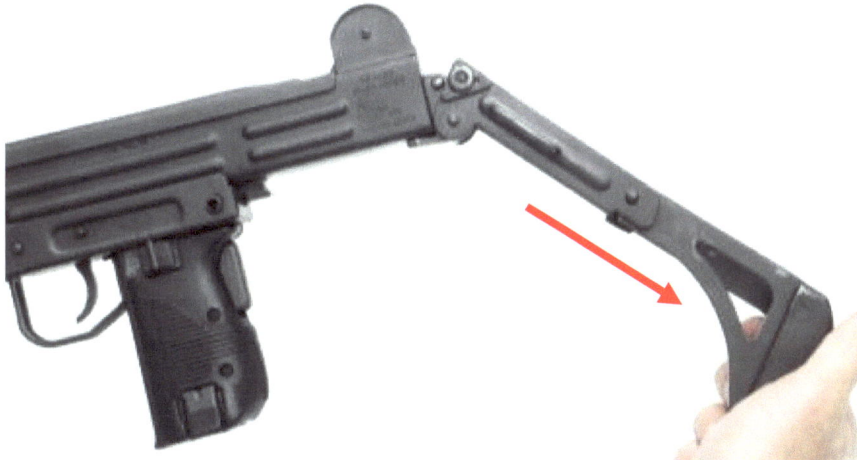

Figure 1-13 Pull the stock until it is locked

Figure 1-13 Rotate the stock up into its fully locked firing position

Folding the stock

Figure 1-13 Press inward against the spring tension on the rear of the stock

Figure 1-13 Folk the rear of the buttstock upwards

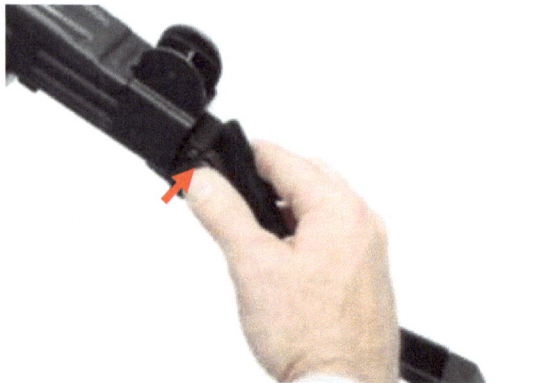

Figure 1-13 Press the forward locking button

Figure 1-13 Place the fold of the stock into the bottom of the receiver

Figure 1-13 Press up on the toe of the stock to lock the stock into the folded position

Loading the UZI

Figure 1-7 Photo of the fire control on SAFE
(A = Automatic, R = Semi-Automatic, and S = SAFE)

1. Once the UZI has been cleared it is ready to be loaded. If being loaded for immediate use you can lock the bolt to the rear with the safety selector on SAFE. If the UZI is to be loaded but not immediately used you may leave the bolt in the forward position and with the safety selector on SAFE, when needed you will have to cock the bolt to the rear with the cocking handle (Figure 2-6).

Figure 2-2a Insert the magazine

Figure 2-2b Fully seat it

2. Insert the magazine into the magazine well and firmly lock it into place. Once inserted and locked you should check the lock by pulling on the magazine to ensure it is fully locked into position (Figures 2-6 and 2-xb).

Figure 2-2a Grasp cocking handle

Figure 2-2b Pull the cocking handle to the rear

Figure 2-2c Release the cocking handle

3. To prepare to fire the UZI from the closed bolt position you must grab the cocking handle, with your finger off the trigger, pull the cocking handle to the rear and release it…the bolt will be retained in the rearward position. Remember this submachine gun fires from the open bolt! (Figures 2-xa through 2-xc).

Mode of Fire Selector Positions

Figure 1-7 Selector is in the middle (AUTOMATIC) position

1. Selector position is fully forward for the weapon to fire in the fully automatic mode, as long as the weapon is loaded, off SAFE and on A, and trigger is pulled fully to the rear the weapon will fire (Figure 2-x).

Figure 1-13 Selector is in the middle (SINGLE SHOT) position

2. Selector position is in the middle position for the weapon to fire in the semi automatic mode, as long as the weapon is loaded, off SAFE, and trigger is pulled fully to the rear and released the weapon will fire single shots (Figure 2-x).

Firing the UZI SMG

Figure 3-23 UZI at the range

1. Orient downrange or towards the threat.

2. If the bolt is forward and the safety engaged you must press the safety with your firing hand thumb to the mode of fire desired (either SEMI or FULL AUTOMATIC) and pull the cocking handle **fully** to the rear with your left hand until it catches the sear. Release the cocking handle and re-grip the forearm of the weapon.

3. As you orient your sights onto the target, press the trigger straight back so as not to interrupt the sight picture. As the UZI is an open bolt weapon, you will notice the movement of the bolt forward once you press the trigger; take this movement into account to maintain your sight alignment and sight picture on the target.

4. For singe shot engagements aim, press, and release the trigger each time as the target requires. For full-automatic bursts, press and hold the trigger to the rear for six- to nine-round bursts and release to reacquire your sights on target. Continue to burst fire as the target requires.

5. When you have completed firing the SMG, place the safety selector into the **"SAFE"** position.

6. To reengage a target from this configuration, press the safety slider to the desired mode of fire, align the sights, and press the trigger for the required type of engagement.

7. You will notice upon firing your last cartridge that the bolt will not return to the rear and will remain forward. Included in the malfunction section of this manual will be is remedial action for failure-to-fire malfunctions due to an empty weapon or dud cartridges.

8. Once firing is completed, clear the weapon as previously detailed in Chapter 2.

Zeroing the UZI

Zero procedure: Attempt to do this on a known distance range on a windless day from a solid bench rest.

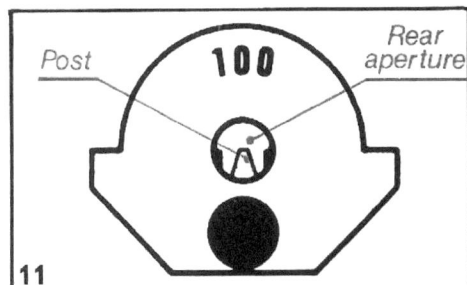

Figure 3-30 100 Meter sight alignment

Sight adjustments are made to the front sight of the UZI.

The front sight consists of a rotating sight post. The front sight will allow you to adjust for elevation by rotating the front sight pin up or down. Note: If you wish to move your point of impact up, then you must rotate the sight down. If you wish your point of impact to go down, you must rotate the front-sight pin up. If you wish to change your windage, then you must drift the windage slide in the opposite direction desired. In general, any changes you make in your front sight must be made in the opposite direction. The standard UZI front-sight tool can be used for elevation correction.

Establish a Zero
1. Distance to target should be 100 meters, and the sight should be set on "100" (for 100 meters).
2. Target should be 12 inches/30 cm high by 8 inches/20 cm, roughly a piece of letter-sized paper on a target silhouette.
3. From a bench or prone position with sandbags for support, carefully aim and fire four round bursts. Ensure proper sight alignment and sight picture and a straight back press of the trigger. If your shots are not striking the point-of-aim, then adjust your sights.
   - To raise the next shot group, rotate the front-sight post in the down direction (clockwise).
   - To lower the next shot group, rotate the front-sight post in the up direction (counter-clockwise).
   - To move the next shot group left, rotate the front sight to the right.
   - To move the next shot group right, rotate the front sight to the left.
   - Continue to fire singe-shots and adjust the sights until you have at least a three out of four hits on the piece of paper.
   - Once this step is done, the SMG is now combat-zeroed. Remember: All shots taken closer than 100 meters will be slightly high but not by more than 3" at extremely close ranges.

Section 2

Maintenance

Figure 2-1 Photo of the overall UZI SMG

Figure 2-2a Photo of the working parts of the UZI SMG

1- Barrel	6- Buttstock	11- Grip Safety
2- Barrel Nut	7- Pistol Grip Assembly	12- Magazine Release Lever
3- Protected Front Sight	8- Magazine	13- Trigger
4- Cocking Handle	9- Forearm	14- Triggerguard
5- Protected Rear Sight	10- Takedown Pin	15- Selector Switch

Clearing the UZI SMG

Figure 2-3 UZI on SAFE

F. Ensure the UZI is on S = "SAFE," and pointed in a safe direction (Figure 2-3).

Figure 2-4a Depress magazine release

Figure 2-4b Remove magazine

G. Remove the magazine by pressing in on the bottom of the magazine release lever (Figure 2-4a) and pull the magazine from the magazine well (Figure 2-4b). Place the magazine in a magazine pouch or set it down.

Figure 2-5 Bolt to the rear

H. If the bolt is locked to the rear; look into the ejection port to visually check the chamber to ensure there is no round in the chamber that failed to be extracted and ejected (Figures 2-5).

Figure 2-6

I. If the bolt is forward you will need to pull the cocking handle to the rear and then look in the ejection port to visually inspect the chamber to ensure there is no round in the chamber that failed to be extracted and ejected (Figure 2-6).

Figure 2-7

J. If you have ensured the magazine is removed and the chamber is clear, while holding rearward pressure on the cocking handle, press the trigger and allow the bolt to move slightly forward. Once the bolt has moved forward 1/4" let go of the trigger and continue to allow the bolt to move forward under your control (Figure 2-7).

Disassembling the UZI SMG

NOTE- Place the UZI's parts on a flat, clean surface with the muzzle oriented in a safe direction.

Once the weapon is cleared and when the operator begins to disassemble the SMG, it should be done in the following order:

Figure 2-8a Hood release

2-8b Press hood release to the rear

1. Press in on the spring loaded receiver cover catch and lift the rear of the receiver cover (Figures 2-8a & 2-8b).

Figure 2-9 Removing the receiver cover

2. Lift off the receiver cover (Figure 2-9).

Figure 2-10 Remove the bolt

3. Press the bolt slightly to the rear and lift it out while maintaining control as it is against the action spring (Figure 2-10).

Figure 2-11 Lift out the bolt

4. Lift out the bolt, driving spring assembly, and buffer up and out of the receiver by lifting up on the front of the bolt (Figure 2-11).

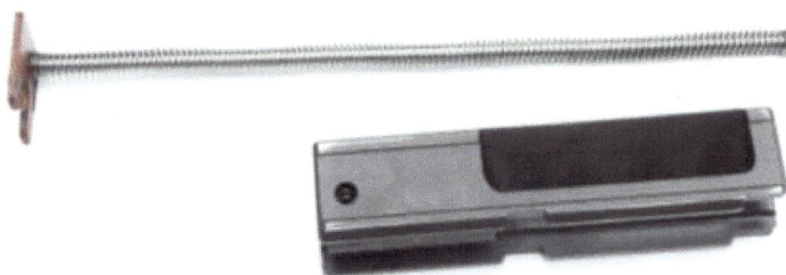

Figure 2-12 Bolt, Driving Spring Assembly and Buffer disassembled

5. Pull the driving spring assembly from the bolt (Figure 2-12).

Figure 2-13a Barrel nut retainer   **2-13b Press in on the retainer**

6. Press in on the barrel nut retainer and unscrew the barrel nut (Figure 2-13b).

Figure 2-14a Remove the barrel nut

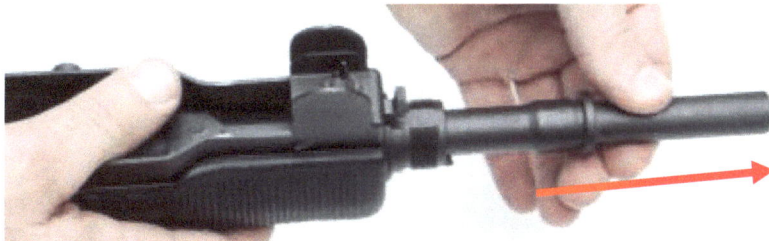

Figure 2-14b Remove the barrel

Figure 2-14c Remove the barrel

7. Once the barrel nut is unscrewed you can remove the nut (Figure 2-14a) and barrel from the receiver (Figures 2-14b and 2-14c).

Figure 2-15 Note the barrel alignment

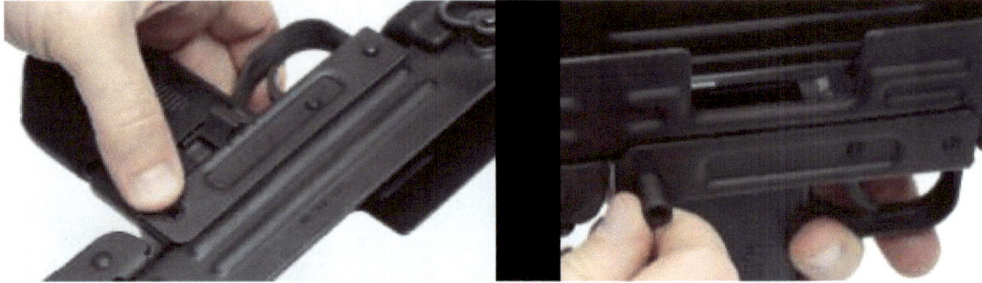

Figure 2-16a	**Figure 2-16b**
Depress the takedown pin and remove it	

8. Depress the takedown pin and remove it (Figures 2-16a and 2-16b).

Figure 2-17 Remove the trigger group assembly

9. Remove the trigger group assembly (Figure 2-17).

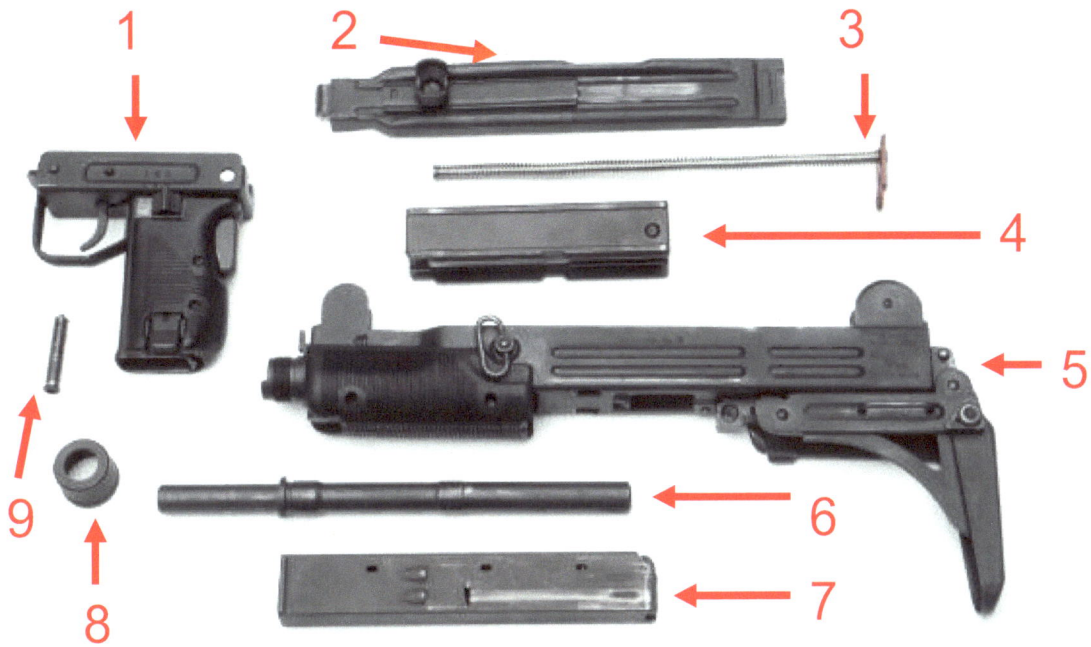

Figure 2-18 Photo of the disassembled UZI SMG

1- Pistol Grip Assembly
2- Top Cover
3- Operating Rod and Spring
4- Bolt
5- Receiver Assembly

6- Barrel
7- Magazine
8- Barrel Nut
9- Takedown Pin

Reassembling the UZI SMG

Reverse the disassembly steps

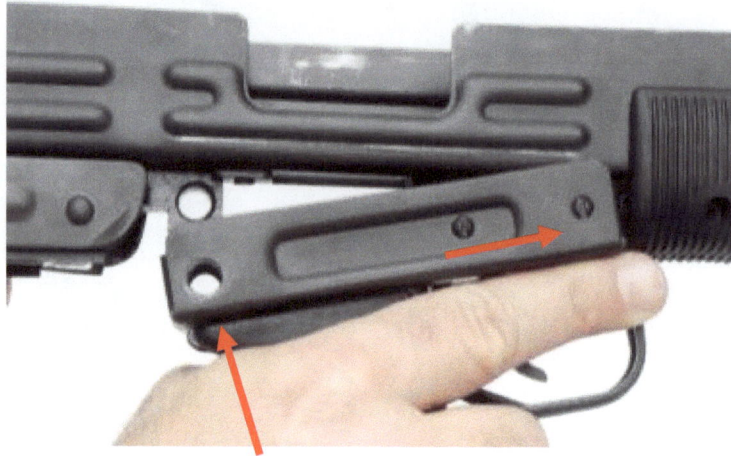

Figure 2-19 Replace the trigger group assembly

1. Place the trigger group assembly front into the receiver and rotate the rear up to align the takedown pin hole (Figure 2-19).

Figure 2-19 Replace the take down pin

2. Push the takedown pin fully in to lock the pistol grip assembly to the receiver (Figure 2-20).

Figure 2-20b Insert the barrel

Figure 2-20a Slide on the barrel nut

3. Slide the barrel into the front of the receiver and turn the barrel until the alignment notch mates with the receiver and then slide on the barrel nut (Figures 2-20a and 2-20b).

Figure 2-21a Screw on the barrel nut **2-21b until the retainer secures the nut**

4. Screw on the barrel nut until it is retained by the barrel nut retainer (Figures 2-21a & 2-21b).

Figure 2-22a Prepare the bolt assembly

Figure 2-22b Insert the bolt

5.   Place the buffer and spring assembly into the bolt then set it into the rear of the receiver, press against the spring and place the bolt down into the receiver (Figure 2-22a and 2-22b).

Figure 2-23a   **Figure 2-23b**

Replace the receiver cover

6.   Place the receiver cover onto the receiver by placing the front of the cover in and then press it down past the spring loaded detent (Figures 2-23a and 2-23b).

Performing a Function Check on the UZI SMG

NOTE- Ensure there is <u>no magazine in the weapon</u>; clear prior to performing a function check.

A. Place the selector to (**SAFE**) is to the full rearward position (**S**).

B. Pull the operating handle fully rearward and release, the bolt should be retained in the rearward position.

C. Press trigger. The bolt should not go forward.

D. Push selector to (**SEMI-AUTOMATIC**) the middle position (**R**).

E. Press the trigger and hold it to the rear. The bolt should go forward. Pull the cocking knob to the rear and the bolt should be retained in the rear. Release the trigger and press it again, the bolt should go forward.

F. Pull the cocking knob to the rear.

G. Push selector to (**FULL-AUTOMATIC**) the forward position (**A**).

H. Press the trigger and hold it to the rear. The bolt should go forward. Pull the cocking knob to the rear and the bolt should not be retained in the rear as you cycle the action replicating full automatic fire.

Maintain pressure on the trigger, and pull the operating handle fully rearward, and release it. The bolt should go forward.

Cleaning the UZI

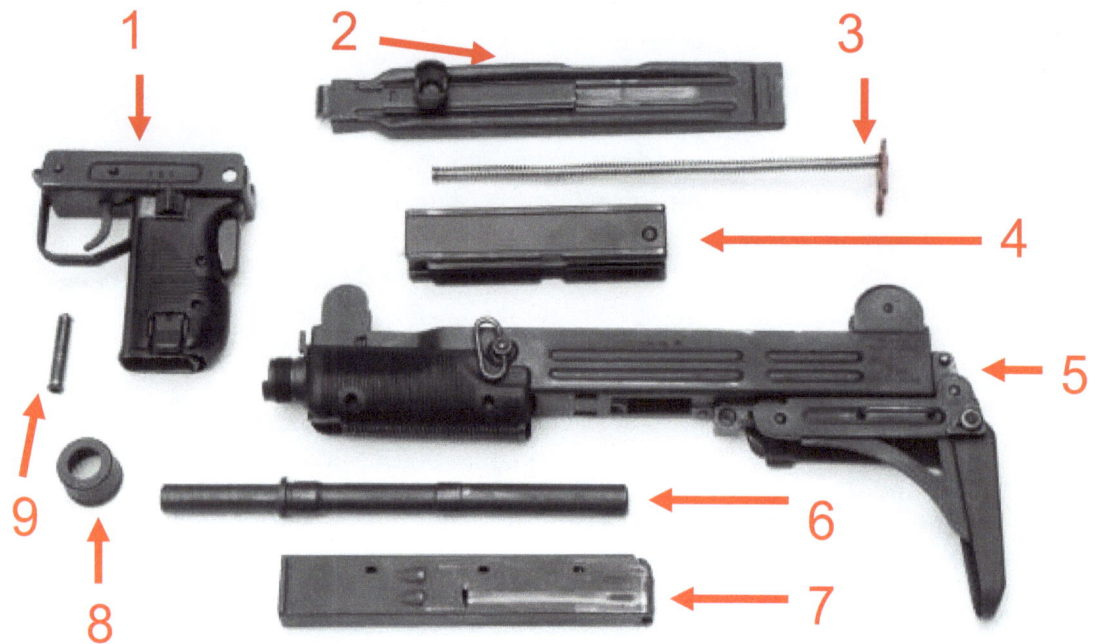

1- Pistol Grip Assembly
2- Top Cover
3- Operating Rod and Spring
4- Bolt
5- Receiver Assembly

6- Barrel
7- Magazine
8- Barrel Nut
9- Takedown Pin

Figure 2-19 Photo of the weapon parts

1. Once fully dissembled into the major groups (stock and receiver, bolt, driving spring assembly and buffer) clean each individual part with a powder solvent (Figure 2-19).

2. Clean the bolt, driving spring assembly and buffer with a powder solvent and dry when completed.

3. Clean the barrel with cleaning rods or a boresnake. Use solvent lubricated brass brushes to break up carbon in the bore, and then use a solvent covered patch to push the carbon out then dry patch until clean. The bores are chromed lined so they clean up easily. A bore snake is a great bore-cleaning product to do this as the barrel is clean with one pass of the bore snake.

4. Once all parts are cleaned they should be inspected for damage. Points to inspect is the condition of the front and rear sights, bolt, firing pin, driving spring assembly, buffer and overall condition of all internal parts.

5. Prior to reassembly of the SMG a light coat of protective oil should be applied to all metal surfaces. Grease should be lightly applied to all the metal surfaces that make contact in the operation of the weapon.

Dissembling the Magazine

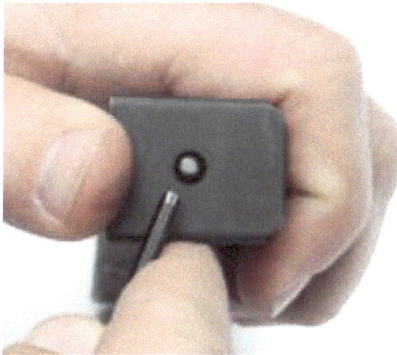

Figure 2-16a Depress floorplate lock

Figure 2-16b Remove floorplate

1. Use a pointed object to depress the retaining plate through the floor plate and start to slide the floor plate to the rear. The older, dirtier, and/or rusty the magazine is, the harder this step will be to do. Be careful not to slide the floor plate fully off until you are ready to apply pressure to the retainer plate, as it is under spring tension (Figures 2-16a and 2-16b).

Figure 2-17a Retain the spring

Figure 2-17b Remove the spring

2. Once you have the floor plate started, use your thumb to hold the retainer plate and remove the floor plate fully. Now you can release the spring tension in a controlled manner and remove the spring and follower from the magazine body. The follower and retaining plate can be removed from the spring if needed for thorough cleaning (Figures 2-17a and 2-17b).

NOTE- It is very important to clean the inside of the magazine body and the outside of the follower. Keep the magazine as dry as possible but lightly coated with a protectant to prevent rusting.

3. To reassemble, just reverse the process.

Section 4

Performance Problems

Malfunction and Immediate Action Procedures

Malfunctions are usually preventable through good practices, but they may still occur out of the blue from time to time. Of course, you hope it is on the practice range, but you should treat each one as if you are in a life-or-death situation. Practicing proper and effective corrective actions will allow you to be more confident in your pistol handling. In stressful situations, you can become much more stressed due to an unforeseen malfunction that is easy to correct. I have observed many shooters that perceive themselves to be experienced, but when they encounter a stovepipe, they nearly disassemble the pistol rather than sweep it out and continue.

Malfunction drills must fix the problem 100% of the time (excluding a weapon stoppage—broken weapon) the first time performed. You must look at the pistol and identify the problem (obviously the pistol is not functioning as you need, so you must transition to another weapon or rectify the situation). It is a non-functioning weapon at this point—fix it.

You should always practice taking a covered position to correct malfunctions with considerations on how you operate.

The following pages in this chapter describe and detail corrective actions for the various malfunctions that may be encountered.

NOTE: The failure-to-go-into-battery malfunction, when your slide does not fully return forward when cycling a round, is always rectified in the same manner, no matter which hand is being used. This malfunction is usually induced when loading and not allowing the full recoil spring tension to shut the slide.

To fix a failure-to-go-into-battery malfunction, you must ensure your finger is off the trigger and outside the triggerguard and then slap the back of the slide with the heel of the non-firing hand. If you are shooting while wounded, then you will use your chest or equipment to force the slide forward into battery.

FAILURE TO FIRE: This malfunction occurs when the operator has loaded a dud cartridge or failed to load the chamber. The universal fix all for this is the "Slap, Rack, Bang" technique.

SYMPTOM - You perform a full presentation to shoot and hear and feel the hammer strike, and the weapon does not fire.

1. SLAP the bottom of the magazine with a hard palm (fingers extended) to ensure it is fully seated and locked in.

2. **RACK** the slide fully to the rear and release it to shut by its own recoil spring tension. You can pivot the slide toward your non-firing hand to assist in racking the slide to the rear; maintain muzzle to threat orientation.

3. **BANG** or represent and prepare to fire the shot as you intended before the malfunction if your situation dictates that action.

FAILURE TO EJECT: This malfunction (commonly called a "stovepipe") is created usually by the bolt being retarded in its rearward movement to rechamber the next round or a broken ejector. This malfunction is easily corrected by sweeping the expended case from the ejection port.

SYMPTOM - You are in the act of shooting a multiple-round engagement, and you felt the bolt did not fully close and/or have a soft mushy trigger.

With the non-firing hand, extend your fingers, and with fingers joined, reach to the cocking knob and pull it to the rear and roll the UZI to the right. (DO NOT SWEEP YOUR HAND IN FRONT OF THE MUZZLE.)

Once the casing is no longer pinched by the bolt, the bolt will lock to the rear and you are now ready to continue the engagement. Continue the engagement as your situation dictates.

FAILURE TO EXTRACT: This malfunction (commonly called a "double feed") is created when the spent casing is not extracted from the chamber, and the next round to be loaded is rammed from the magazine into the rear of the stuck casing. This malfunction is a serious one since more complicated dexterity is needed to correct it and, of course, to do it quickly. Below is the breakdown of the corrective action to restore your UZI back to operation.

SYMPTOM - You are shooting a multiple-shot engagement and notice your bolt did not go forward, you have a soft mushy trigger, and it will not fire.

STEP ONE - With your finger off the trigger, rotate the UZI to the right and rack the cocking knob to the rear and lock the bolt to the rear.

STEP TWO - Remove the magazine from the UZI.

STEP THREE - Rack the slide to the rear at least two times to ensure the casing is extracted and ejected from the UZI, keep pointed in a safe direction as the stuck round may fire. As you are doing this step, observe the casing being ejected and allow the slide to use its force to shut each time it is pulled to the rear. Once the round is clear of the chamber now lock the bolt to the rear.

STEP FOUR - Properly insert and seat a loaded magazine with a hard palm.

STEP FIVE - Your UZI is now ready to continue the engagement as the situation dictates.

NOTE: Correcting this malfunction needs to be practiced often since it is the most complicated to do under stress or when you lose dexterity because blood is leaving the extremities.

www.ingramcontent.com/pod-product-compliance
Lightning Source LLC
Chambersburg PA
CBHW061057090426
42742CB00002B/76